THE LAST LEGAL SPITBALL AND OTHER LITTLE-KNOWN FACTS ABOUT SPORTS

ƶ

THE LAST LEGAL SPITBALL AND OTHER LITTLE-KNOWN FACTS ABOUT SPORTS

Written and Illustrated by Barbara Seuling

Doubleday & Company, Inc.
Garden City, New York

Copyright © 1975 by Barbara Seuling
All Rights Reserved
Printed in the United States of America
9   8   7   6   5   4   3   2

Library of Congress Cataloging in Publication Data

Seuling, Barbara.
   The last legal spitball and other little-known facts about sports.

   SUMMARY: Includes such obscure sports facts as: The word "love"
used in tennis scoring is derived from the French "l'oeuf" meaning
egg or zero.
   1.   Sports—Juvenile literature. [1.   Sports]   I.   Title.
GV707.S45   1974   796
ISBN 0-385-08412-9
ISBN 0-385-09976-2 (prebound)
Library of Congress Catalog Card Number 73–14056

For my Mother

The most stolen bases in a lifetime was 892, by Tyrus R. ("Ty") Cobb, of the Detroit Tigers, between 1905 and 1926 and the Philadelphia Athletics in 1927 and 1928. Thirty-two of those were for stealing home.

The forerunner of the sport basketball was an
Aztec game with a solid rubber ball and a stone
ring placed high on a wall. The winner was
entitled to the clothing of all the spectators, while
the loser often was executed.

When Connie Mack arrived as manager of the
Philadelphia Athletics in 1901 he had no
players and no ball park. The Athletics were called
"a white elephant," and wore this as a symbol on
their uniforms for years.

Dick Sheppard of Gloucester, England, rode his
motorcycle through a 35-foot-long tunnel of fire
on September 21, 1968.

A New York City hotel boasted a special 8½×6½
foot bed for basketball players, but at the special
promotional exhibit the guest of honor, 7-foot
1-inch Wilt Chamberlain, did not show up.

Lou Gehrig of the New York Yankees played in
2,130 consecutive games.

David Kwan, 22, averaged 32 miles a day walking from Singapore to London. He covered 18,500 miles in 81 weeks.

Spread over a period of 23 days, it is estimated that more than 10 million spectators watch the annual *Tour de France* cycle race along the route.

Jockey Willy Shoemaker won more than 6,000 races in his lifetime.

The Encylopedia of Sports Sciences and Medicine reports that football is the most dangerous game in the world. It also reports that the end run in high school football causes more injuries than any other play; that training exercises such as full squats and duck waddles are bad for the joints; that if pep talks are legitimate to inspire athletes, so is hypnosis.

It is rare for a professional hockey player to have his own teeth. Most players have had theirs knocked out early in their careers.

A football game between Washington State College
and San Jose State College in 1955 drew one paying
customer. The game was played in near-zero
temperature.

George Halas of the Chicago Bears ran 98 yards with a recovered fumble, a record that stood for 49 years. And he did it with Jim Thorpe chasing him.

The marathon is based on the legend of Pheidippides, who ran 26 miles from Marathon to Athens to announce a victory over the invading Persians. On his arrival and announcement, he fell dead. After the 1972 Olympics, champion Frank Shorter remarked, exhausted, that he wished Pheidippides had dropped after the 22nd mile.

Ninety-seven-year-old Rebecca Lacy of Cloverdale, Oregon, caught 72 salmon at the age of 72, and her biggest fish, a 47-pound Chinook, in her 96th year.

In the first basketball games, a ladder was used to retrieve the ball from the basket after scoring.

The Vasa Lopp ski race in Sweden draws more participants than any other competitive sport event in the world. In 1972, there were 8,500 entries.

Sandy Koufax of the Los Angeles Dodgers made history in 1965 with 382 strike-outs in one season. In 1886, pitcher Matthew Kilroy of the Baltimore American Association team had more strike-outs—505—but the distance from the mound to the batter was 10½ feet shorter.

The toughest automobile race is said to be the Targa Florio in Sicily, which covers 11 laps (492.126 miles) of harrowing mountain roads involving 9,350 corners.

The longest hit in the major leagues was by Mickey
Mantle of the New York Yankees, in 1953. His
home run measured 565 feet.

The highest speed of a ball in any team game is 160 miles per hour in pelota (jai-alai).

On his reinduction into the Basketball Hall of Fame, UCLA's coach Johnny Wooden read a news item printed twenty-five years before, which read "due to the unavailability of a prominent coach, Mr. Wooden will be the substitute speaker." Wooden is believed to be the first person to be twice enshrined in the same Hall of Fame —once as a player and again as a coach.

The last legal spitball was thrown by Burleigh Grimes in 1934. Although the spitball was outlawed in baseball's major leagues in 1920, all spitball pitchers were permitted to throw this pitch until the end of their careers, and Grimes lasted for fourteen more years.

The word "love" meaning "no score" in the game of tennis is derived from the French word for egg (zero, zilch, goose egg), "l'oeuf."

When Yogi Berra was a New York Yankee he played in more World Series than any other player—a total of 14.

In an automobile duration test in 1963, a West German Ford Taunus was driven the equivalent of 8.93 times around the equator, or 222,618 miles.

Only two jockeys have ever won the Kentucky Derby five times: Eddie Arcaro in 1938, 1941, 1945, 1948, and 1952; and Bill Hartack in 1957, 1960, 1962, 1964, and 1969.

In his first major league game on August 23, 1936, Bob Feller, Cleveland Indians pitcher, struck out 15 St. Louis Browns players, something that had not been done for 17 years in the American League. Exactly 3 weeks later he struck out 17 Philadelphia Athletics, tying Dizzy Dean's record.

In 1972, Frank Shorter was the first American since 1908 to win the Olympic marathon. During a winter cross-country championship contest previous to that, Shorter wore panty-hose to keep out the cold.

Seven-foot three-inch Vasiliy Akhtayev of the U.S.S.R. was the tallest basketball player of all time. The tallest U.S. professional player is Kareem Abdul Jabbar, who measures 7 feet 1⅜ inches tall. Latvia boasts the tallest woman player, Ulyana Semyonova, who stands 6 feet 9½ inches.

Mountain climbing as a sport caught on as far
back as the sixteenth century. Leonardo da Vinci
was known to have taken part in expeditions up
the southern slopes of the Pennines.

When Tom Burleson was measured for the 1972
U. S. Olympic basketball team at 7 feet 2¼ inches,
1¾ inches shorter than his recorded height, he
remarked: "After all, I'm 7 feet 4 inches with my
shoes on, and I never play barefooted."

In 1936, at the age of 13, Marjorie Gestring took the springboard diving title at the Berlin Olympics, becoming the youngest individual Olympic winner.

Gary Gabelich attained the fastest land speed ever—627.027 m.p.h.—on the Bonneville Salt Flats in Utah on October 23, 1970. He did it in the *Blue Flame*, a four-wheeled vehicle powered by liquid natural gas.

M. Frank ("Pinky") Higgins, of the Boston Red Sox, made 12 hits in succession on June 19, 1938, in two games. Walter Dropo of the Detroit Tigers equalled the record on July 14 and 15, 1952, also in two games.

The New York Giants stole the most bases in one season—in 1911—with 347 in 154 games.

The Washington Senators stole 8 bases in the first inning of a game on July 19, 1915. The Philadelphia Phillies did it also in the ninth inning of a game on July 7, 1919.

Bill Daniels, owner of the ABA Utah Stars, likes to drive from Denver to Salt Lake City—about ten hours—so he can get away from the telephone.

On December 9, 1934, the New York Giants won the football championship over the undefeated Chicago Bears 30–13, and most of the credit was given to the sneakers the Giants wore to keep their footing on the frozen turf.

In the earliest recorded games, in 776 B.C., a
cook named Coroebus was the first winner in a
foot race.

On January 7, 1785, a French pilot, Jean-Pierre
Blanchard and an American doctor, John Jeffries,
left Dover, England, in a balloon, hoping to cross
the English Channel. The balloon started to leak
and sink, so everything possible went overboard,
including biscuits, coats, and Blanchard's pants.
They finally landed safely, in the treetops of
Calais, across the Channel.

24

In amateur wrestling, before modern rules were employed, wrestlers could be locked in holds for so long that bouts could last 11 hours.

Karate expert Hirokazu Kanazawa, the only winner of two All-Japanese titles, won the first title with a broken arm.

French records from 300 years ago show pictures of a diver equipped with flippers and an air cylinder—very similar to today's modern scuba equipment.

The only NHL rookie ever to score hat tricks in consecutive games is Steve Vickers of the New York Rangers.

Mike Coons of the Schoharie, New York, Central High basketball team played with a wooden leg strapped to his thigh. He averaged only 2 points a game, but his teammates loved having him on the team because he was an inspiration to them.

In the Futurity Races, horses are entered in races before they are born.

The youngest person ever to break a world swimming record was Karen Yvette Muir of South Africa. At the age of 12 she broke the women's 110-yard backstroke world record with 1 minute 08.7 seconds.

"Crestfallen," now used as a term for one who
seems defeated or disappointed, came into use
from cockfights: the loser was the cock with the
fallen crest.

The greatest earnings of a baseball player were the $1,091,477 amassed by Babe Ruth between 1914 and 1938. It wasn't until 1935 that income tax laws were passed, so Ruth was able to keep most of the money he made.

The game of basketball as we know it began in 1891 when Dr. James Naismith of the Springfield, Massachusetts, Training School of the International Y.M.C.A. College nailed a peach basket up on the side of his barn and threw a soccer ball into it.

The speed of a golf ball driven off a tee has been electrically timed at about 170 m.p.h.

In 1925, the New York Giants were worth $500 to the NFL. Today, the Giants' franchise is estimated to be worth close to $20 million.

The "Georgia Peach," Ty Cobb, baseball's greatest player, who set 90 records (10 of which still stand) during his 25-year career, couldn't bat in a single run in three World Series.

Some of Ty Cobb's records were: for playing in the most games (3,033); for making the most base hits (4,191); for stealing the most bases (892); and for having a lifetime average of .367.

Charles Zibbelman of the United States swam continuously for 168 hours in a Honolulu swimming pool. Mr. Zibbelman is legless.

The largest audience assembled to watch one basketball exhibition was a crowd of 75,000 in West Berlin, to see the Harlem Globetrotters.

The shortest baseball game was 51 minutes long, on September 28, 1919, between the New York Giants and the Philadelphia Phillies.

The longest game by time was 7.23 hours long and lasted 23 innings. It was between the San Francisco Giants and the New York Mets, on May 31, 1964.

Professional divers thrill crowds by diving from a 118-foot cliff in Acapulco, Mexico. The water they dive into is only 12 feet deep, and the base rocks extend out 21 feet, so the divers must calculate incoming waves, and still jump 27 feet forward.

Mike Souchak shot the lowest 72-hole score on a first-class golf course—257 (27 under par)—in the Texas Open at San Antonio in February 1955.

Sonja Henie, Norwegian Olympic figure skating
champion and Hollywood movie star, amassed
a fortune of $47,500,000 in her career, making her
the wealthiest skater the world has known.

The Jockey Club, one of England's most
prestigious and exclusive private clubs, recently
elected the first real jockey to its membership in
its total existence of 220 years.

The Detroit Institute of Technology dropped five basketball players, a manager, and a publicity worker because of poor grades in the 1971–72 season. The immediate result was a 110–30 loss to Guelph.

The Reverend James Curtin of Walsall, England, used his parishioners' Christmas gift to him of a special collection to bet on football, and won $100,000. Another clergyman in Rome was not so fortunate. He allowed someone else to get ahead of him at the lottery counter, and that person's $.80 ticket won $192,000.

On December 23, 1962, the Dallas Texans played the Houston Oilers in "football's longest day"—the championship game that lasted 77 minutes 54 seconds. In an unprecedented six quarters, Dallas won 20–17.

The longest cycle tour was made by Mishreelal Jaiswal of India, through 107 countries, covering 135,000 miles. It took him 14 years, and he wore out 5 machines.

In 1916, Georgia Tech set a school scoring record in football by beating Cumberland College in Lebanon, Tennessee, by 222–0.

Three hundred and sixty-four pound Paul Anderson of the United States can lift 6,290 pounds on his back.

When golf pro Jack Nicklaus asked baseball pro Henry Aaron what kind of golfer he was, Aaron replied: "It took me 17 years to get 3,000 hits in baseball. I did it in one afternoon on the golf course."

34

When the major league clubs failed to grant him a
tryout, 69-year-old Perry P. Glass petitioned the
Supreme Court to hear his case. He had already
shown his determination when the Atlanta Braves
refused to answer his requests, and even gave him
a child's pass to all games for being in his "second
childhood." Perry responded by standing on his
head atop the Braves' dugout.

The heaviest football player known was 447-pound
Bob Pointer, tackle for the 1967 Santa Barbara High
School team in California.

In June 1973, Secretariat not only won the Triple Crown, the first horse to do so in 25 years, but won the Belmont Stakes by a record-breaking 31 lengths, in a time of 2:24.

Babe Ruth of the New York Yankees slugged in more home runs in a single World Series game than any other player—3. It happened twice, in the 1926 season, and again in 1928.

Skater Kenneth LeBel jumped over 17 barrels in Liberty, New York, on January 9, 1965.

In the first professional football game, on August 31, 1895, when Latrobe, Pennsylvania, played the neighboring town of Jeanette, the quarterback, John Brailler, was paid $10 for being on the Latrobe team. Brailler later became a dentist.

The New York Mets were the only team in history to lose 737 baseball games in only 7 years. In 1962 alone, they lost 120 games. However, in their eighth year, after being the laughing stock of professional baseball, they not only won the pennant, but annihilated the Baltimore Orioles in the 1969 World Series.

The Mets acquired pitcher Tom Seaver, 25-game winner and Cy Young Award winner, in a raffle. In 1965, Seaver had signed a $50,000 bonus contract with the Milwaukee Braves, but it violated the rules, having been signed after the season started. Therefore, Seaver was raffled off, and the Mets won him.

When Casey Stengel agreed to manage the Mets, on September 29, 1961, he talked about how happy he was to be running the New York Knickerbockers. It was half an hour at least before he realized they were the Mets.

Mets manager Casey Stengel showed up in the wrong city (New York) for a big draft meeting (in Cincinnati).

The Mets lost one game on account of snow—on a Palm Sunday.

In 1892, big gloves were used for the first time when James J. Corbett defeated John L. Sullivan in 21 rounds, at New Orleans.

The yo-yo endurance record was won by David Rose at Hereford, England, on June 23, 1970. He yo-yoed for 8 hours and 32 minutes.

Eight-year-old Joy Foster won the Jamaican singles and mixed-doubles championship in Ping-pong in 1958, making her the youngest person ever to win international honors.

Vauxhall Motors' basketball team arrived late for the 1972 National Championship semi-final game because their Vauxhall motor coach broke down.

Americans first started skiing when "Snowshoe" Thompson of Norway introduced skiing to California in the mid-1800s. Englishmen became interested in skiing as a sport when Sir Arthur Conan Doyle, author of the Sherlock Holmes stories, wrote about a ski journey.

The Boston Celtics hold the NBA record for the most points scored in one game—173.

In 1937, Lillian Leitzel of the U.S. did 27 one-hand chin-ups, setting a women's world record.

Kitty Giesler of the United States dove a record-breaking 325 feet, using scuba equipment, off the Bahamas in 1967. In the same place in the same year, Evelyn Patterson of Zambia also broke a record by diving 125 feet, using no equipment at all—just holding her breath.

Ernie Nevers of the Chicago Cardinals holds the NFL record for the most points scored in a game —forty.

No matter when they were actually born, all race horses become a year older on January 1.

The shortest world-title fight was in New York on April 6, 1914, when Al McCoy knocked out George Chip in 45 seconds, winning the middleweight crown.

Gerald Cheevers of the Cleveland Crusaders hockey team paints his goal-tender's mask with imaginary stitchmarks, to remind himself that his face would look like that if he didn't wear a mask.

The longest time a person has been able to stay
under water holding one's breath is 13 minutes
42.5 seconds.

On November 12, 1859, acrobat Jules Léotard
introduced the flying trapeze at a circus in Paris.
He also introduced his costume, which is still
being worn today by acrobats and dancers, and
which bears his name, the *leotard*.

44

Probably the most important seconds in boxing history occurred in Philadelphia on September 23, 1926, during the Gene Tunney/Jack Dempsey fight for the heavyweight championship. Both fighters had agreed before the bout to a new rule, that anyone scoring a knockdown must go to the farthest neutral corner, at which point the referee would begin the count. In the 7th round Dempsey knocked Tunney to the floor but went to the wrong corner. Seconds passed as the referee shouted the new rule to Dempsey and Dempsey moved to the proper corner. The referee started the count, and the instant before he called "10" Tunney got to his feet. Somehow he pulled himself together, rallied, and in the 10th round floored Dempsey, winning the fight.

The first English description of surfing was recorded in 1779 by a member of Captain Cook's exploring party in Hawaii. He called it "most perilous" and "altogether astonishing."

In 1972 swimmer Mark Spitz of California was the
first person in history to win 7 gold Olympic medals.
In addition to winning the medals, he had set or
helped set world records in each of his 7 races.
When he was only 10, Spitz had already set a U.S.
record in the 50-yard butterfly.

Joe Louis successfully defended the heavyweight
championship 25 times between 1937 and 1948.
In 26 bouts he had 22 knockouts.

"Merrick," an American race horse, had the
longest life span of any registered horse—38 years.

During his first season of football, in junior high,
Y. A. Tittle, the great quarterback, only played
until a replacement shoe was sent in for the
regular player—a total of two minutes.

Golf balls in the mid-nineteenth century were made of feathers, stuffed into a little leather bag and sewn closed.

Coach Bill Gibson of Virginia had his basketball
team, the Cavaliers, practice all week with cotton
in their ears to keep out crowd noises. They still lost.

48

Iowa State coach Maury John hired an organist and sent him to Des Moines to pick up some tips on how to fire up State basketball players and fans with rallying tunes.

In one 9-inning game against the Chicago White Sox on October 2, 1949, the St. Louis Browns used 9 pitchers.

In ancient days fighters spat on their hands to increase the strength of their blows, because spit was considered magical.

The first automobile race was from Paris to Versailles and back, about 20 miles, on April 20, 1887. It was won by Georges Bouton who averaged a speed of 16.22 miles per hour in his steam vehicle.

As early as 1786, "baste-ball," a forerunner of the modern game of baseball, was banned in Princeton, New Jersey.

During the days preceding the 1970–71 Cotton Bowl, in which the Texas Longhorns were to play Notre Dame, a sign in front of a church in Dallas read:

God is impartial.

We are not.

Hook'em, Horns.

One of the members of the University of Michigan's first basketball team, in 1908–09, was Gregory Peck, Sr., father of the movie star.

In early football, a team from Massillon, Ohio, signed 45 players for one game so that not a single good player would be left for the opposing team.

Chuck Connors, TV star of *The Rifleman* series, once played baseball for the Chicago Cubs and the Brooklyn Dodgers.

Jeff Tebbs, Utah State basketball star, saved a choking baby by turning her upside down and patting her on the back. Luckily, he did not have to use mouth-to-mouth rescuscitation: Tebbs' jaw had been broken in a recent game and was wired shut.

A clergyman in Monroe, North Carolina, teaches judo in his spare time. He is reported to have remarked: "I teach what to do after you've turned both cheeks."

The longest boxing match with gloves lasted 110 rounds, in 7 hours and 19 minutes. It was between Andy Bowen and Jack Burke in New Orleans on April 6–7, 1893. The greatest number of rounds was 278, in the Jack Jones/Patsey Tunney fight in 1825, which Jones won.

Bronko Nagurski received $210.43 for helping the Chicago Bears win their first NFL championship playoff in 1933. Thirty years later Larry Glueck got $5,899 for the same work when the Bears again won the championship.

Erich Segal, author of *Love Story*, competes every year in the Boston Marathon. In 1972 he came in 694th.

In 1880, the rules of baseball required 9 balls to walk a player.

The only goalie ever to score a goal in professional hockey was Michael Plasse of the Kansas City Blues of the Central Hockey League. He blocked a shot by the Oklahoma Blazers, flipped it up toward the Oklahoma net, and right into the enemy goal.

Auburn University's Dr. Wayne Shell announced
his theory that fish lose their appetites when they
are worried about their sex lives, and therefore
do not nibble at fishermen's bait.

Johnny Unitas, the former star quarterback for the Baltimore Colts holds the NFL record for the most football passes ever completed. He also holds the NFL record for the most fumbles in a career.

The five leading jockeys of 1970 were all either from Panama (3) or Puerto Rico (2).

In Austria there are approximately 60,000 car accidents a year, and 70,000 ski accidents. One out of every seven people ski.

Babe Ruth, chided about the fact that his $80,000 salary was higher than President Herbert Hoover's, supposedly remarked, "Well, I had a better year."

It is estimated that half the adults in Switzerland are skiers.

Gus Johnson of the Baltimore Bullets has smashed three glass backboards during play.

Alf Dean caught a 2,664-pound man-eating shark off the coast of Australia in 1959, the largest rod-caught fish on record.

A tug of war in Jubbulpore, India, on August 12, 1889, lasted 2 hours and 41 minutes. The winning team moved a net distance of 12 feet at an average speed of 0.00084 miles per hour.

Referees had to plead for time out to catch their breaths and relieve cramped legs four times during the 1972 basketball season of Oral Roberts University. The swift-paced team, top scorers of the year, averaged 105.1 points per game.

People once bowled in churches, believing that a "strike" was a holy sign of a good life.

In the Super Bowl game of 1972–73, President Nixon suggested a play to coach Don Shula of the Miami Dolphins. The play, a long down-and-in pass from Bob Griese to Paul Warfield, was executed. It didn't work and may have cost the Dolphins the game.

The longest NFL field goal, 63 yards, was kicked by Tom Dempsey of the New Orleans Saints on November 8, 1970, for a 19–17 victory over the Detroit Lions. It broke a standing record of 17 years by 7 yards. Dempsey, born with only a stub of a hand and a partial foot, never believed he was handicapped.

Dudley Morton, the junior center of Tennessee
State, did not show up for his team's quarter-final
basketball contest in the 1972 NCAA Tournament
in Evansville because he could not find a baby-sitter
and had to stay home and look after his two
children.

59

The American Medical Association reports that
46 per cent of all college football players are
injured during the season, half seriously enough
to qualify for the hospital or the bench in
the next game. It is also reported that 67 per cent
of all injuries occur in the second and third
quarters.

Thirteen-year-old Debbie Andresne, of Muscatine, Iowa, bowled a 288 game for her local Junior-Senior League.

On February 6, 1971, Alan Shephard made history by not only walking on the moon, but by swinging a 6-iron at some golf balls up there. He missed the first, taking a mulligan, which won him a lifetime membership in the U. S. Duffers Association of Newport, Kentucky. The organization also awarded Shephard the presidency of their first moon chapter.

The oldest person to ever hold a world title was Pierre Etchbaster, at 60 years, who retired in 1955 after 27 years as undefeated world amateur tennis champion.

Chess was invented in India in the seventh century, and was played as a game of war, to learn about army movements. More recently, the Russians trained their soldiers for war with chess.

The fastest skier flies along at more than 100 m.p.h.

Emperor Ming Huang (716–756) was an avid polo player, but he always demanded the game be played on mules.

On January 25, 1972, German-born John Tuszynski of Southern Methodist flew from Dallas to Galesburg, Illinois, his home town, then drove fifty miles to Peoria where he took his naturalization oath, then flew back to Dallas and played in a basketball game between the Mustangs and Arkansas.

At the Shawnee Invitational for Ladies at
Shawnee-on-Delaware, Pennsylvania, in about
1912, a woman set a record by completing the
short 130-yard 16th hole in more strokes than
anyone else—166. Most of the balls ended up in
the Binniekill River. The woman's name is
unknown, of course.

Some zoos, such as New York's Bronx Zoo, put TV sets in gorillas' cages to relieve their boredom. A survey reports that TV-watching gorillas prefer love scenes, weight lifting, and auto racing to any other programs.

Oscar Robertson led Cincinnati in both points and assists in every one of his 10 seasons with the basketball club.

The greatest sports arena of all time, the Colosseum in Rome, once held more than 50,000 spectators. Today it is abandoned, inhabited only by thousands of cats.

In 1924, Forest Peters of Montana State University drop-kicked 17 field goals in one game.

The expression "throw in the sponge" came from boxing.

The first roller-skating rink in the world was built in Newport, Rhode Island, in 1866.

The longest ski lift in the world, in the Snowy Mountains of Australia, ascends 3.5 miles and takes about an hour to reach the top.

Golfer Sam Snead won 4 consecutive PGA titles.

In the nineteenth century a prize of $10,000 was offered to find a substitute for ivory in billiard balls. Celluloid was first substituted, but today's balls are made of cast resin.

American professional golfers are said to be the highest paid athletes in the world. Arnold Palmer and Jack Nicklaus reportedly earn around a million dollars a year from combined prize money, endorsements, and business activities—some of which have nothing to do with golf.

An unlosable golf ball was invented by a
businessman, Stephen Horchler, of Scotland. It
contains a tiny radio transmitter, and bleeps
distress signals.

Cincinnati pitcher Joe Nuxhall began his career in June 1944, at the age of 15, making him the youngest major league player on record.

The Indiana State Reformatory advertised as follows in the Reformatory newspaper, addressed to state judges, prosecutors, and policemen: *The Indiana Reformatory varsity baseball and softball teams are in dire need of league players . . . especially pitchers. Would you please oblige us?*

In the Philadelphia Phillies-Pittsburgh Pirates game of July 10, 1929, a home run was hit in every inning.

A 4-year-old boy, Craig Kunch, placed 4th in a La Jolla, California, surfing competition. The other contestants were twice his age or more.

The lowest golf score on record for an 18-hole course, par 70 or more, is 55, achieved by A. E. Smith of Woolacombe, England, in 1936, on his 4,248-yard home course. Homero Blancas matched that score on the 5,002-yard Premier Golf Course in Longview, Texas, in 1962.

The heaviest wrestler of all time was 802-pound "Happy Humphrey," William J. Cobb of Macon, Georgia.

The most stolen bases in a single game by one person was 7, by George F. ("Piano Legs") Gore, of the Chicago Nationals, on June 25, 1881, and by William R. ("Sliding Billy") Hamilton of the Philadelphia Phillies on August 31, 1894.

Jim Clark won more Grand Prix races than any other driver—25. He had 7 victories in 1963 alone.

The last championship bare knuckles bout was in 1889, between John L. Sullivan and Jake Kilrain. Sullivan won, in 75 rounds.

John Mayson of Lincoln University took an inbounds pass and drove for an unmolested layup —into the wrong basket. His team lost 66–60 to Delaware State.

Chick Linster, 16, of Wilmette, Illinois, did 6,006 consecutive push-ups.

It is estimated that the French national economy suffers a loss of about $720,000,000 during the annual *Tour de France* bicycle race, which runs over 3,569 miles and lasts 29 days. The loss is based on the fact that one third of the working population works only two thirds of the time during the race.

During the late 1800s, Brooklynites called themselves "trolley-dodgers," after their fear of swift-moving streetcars, so the name "Dodgers" came naturally when they had to name their baseball team. Now the team is in Los Angeles, where there are no streetcars.

Shenandoah College basketball coach Michael
Kolsky double-checks the referees with homemade
video tapes. Once he got the officials to review the
last play of a game and they agreed to alter their
decision.

In one of the most extraordinary hitting performances in baseball, Ed Delahanty of the Philadelphia Phillies slugged home runs to left, right, and center, plus one inside-the-park in one game. It happened on July 13, 1896, and Delahanty was given four sticks of chewing gum for his work.

The St. Louis Cardinals famous pitching brothers, Dizzy and Daffy Dean, won 49 regular games and 4 World Series games between them in 1934.

The U.S. has won every America's Cup international yacht championship since the competition's inception in 1851.

On New Year's night, about one million people (more than 20 per cent of the population) of São Paulo, Brazil, turn out for the annual San Sylvestre road race through the streets of the city.

Johnny Weissmuller, winner of 3 gold medals for swimming in the 1924 Olympics, promoted bathing suits before he won the part of Tarzan over 75 others who auditioned for the role.

Vern Mikkelsen of the Minneapolis Lakers fouled out of 127 NBA games, a career record.

It is estimated that the smash of Chinese champion Ping-pong player Chuang Tse-tung flies at more than 60 m.p.h.

Robert L. Douglas, manager of the Renaissance Casinos since 1922, was elected to the Basketball Hall of Fame in 1972 as the winningest coach in basketball history, the first black honored with Hall of Fame recognition, and the oldest man ever elected.

The referee was attacked and killed by a fighting bird during a cockfight in Manila.

Skis have been found in European bogs dating back to about 2500 B.C.

French tightrope walker Jean François Gravelet
crossed Niagara Falls on July 30, 1855, on a rope
160 feet above the Falls. He repeated the feat
five years later, this time carrying his agent on his
back.

Sky-divers can fall at a speed of 185 m.p.h. in a head-down free-falling position.

When Johnny Unitas was out of college and looking for a job in football, professional teams passed him up in more than 200 draft choices and he played a year of semi-pro football before the Colts finally decided to take a chance on him.

In 1898, during a game in Philadelphia, third-base coach Tommy Corcoran of the Cincinnati Reds was scuffing around in the dirt, and his spikes caught on something. Thinking it was a vine, he dug it up with his toe and trailed it. It led to the Phillie clubhouse, where he found Morgan Murphy, the Phillie catcher, equipped with a pair of opera glasses and a telegraph buzzer. He had been stealing and relaying signals to the third-base Phillie coach.

New York Giants' coach Alex Webster threatened to sue Jim Bouton and New York's WABC-TV for $1,500,000 for running an interview on TV without sound, making him look like "a dullard and a stupid person." The station claims it was an accident, but Bouton remarked that he had really intended to run the interview backward.

As early as the fifteenth century, billiards was recorded in a poem by French poet Clément Marot.

Forty-one-year-old James R. Beads of Maryland ran non-stop for 22½ hours in October 1969, covering 121 miles, 440 yards.

The first badminton birdie was a champagne cork stuck with feathers.

The world's spitting champion, Don Sydner of the United States, achieved a distance of 25 feet 10 inches. He received a gold-plated spittoon as his prize.

BARBARA SEULING, a native New Yorker, studied art and literature at Columbia University. She has spent most of her time since as an editor, illustrator, and writer, except for working one summer at the World's Fair in 1963, where her office was directly over a nuclear fission display, accompanied by a large "BOOM!" precisely every four minutes. She lives in Manhattan. This is her third children's book.